SONGS OF PRAISE

Toccata for Organ

Robert Prizeman

CHESTER MUSIC

SONGS OF PRAISE
Toccata for Organ

Robert Prizeman

© Copyright 1986, 1994 for all countries
Chester Music Ltd., 8/9 Frith Street, London W1V 5TZ

CH 55835

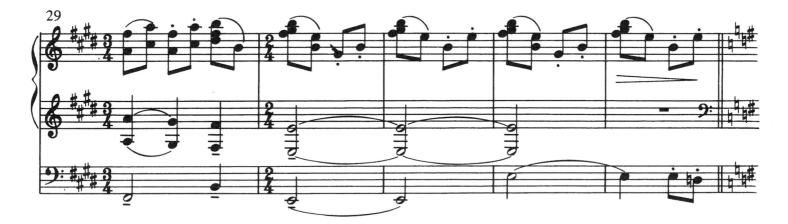

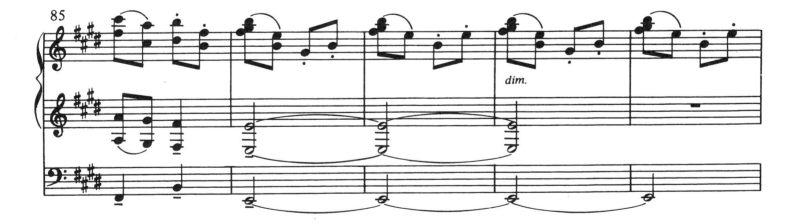

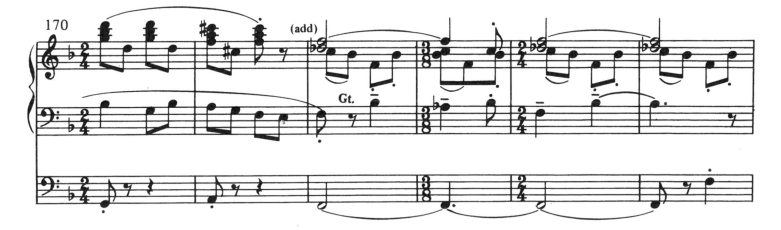

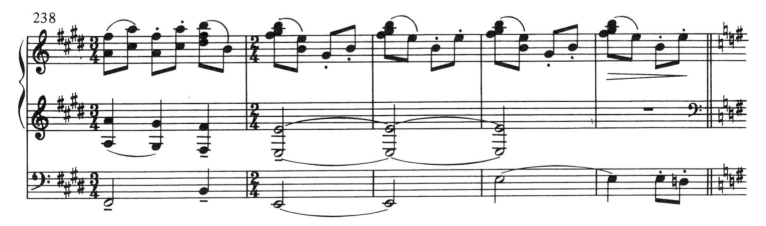

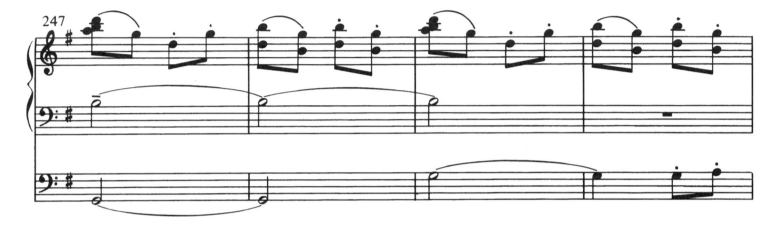